REAL WORLD DATA

GRAPHING
CHANGING LANDSCAPES

Andrew Solway

Heinemann
LIBRARY

Chicago, Illinois

Edited by Nancy Dickmann, Rachel Howells,
    and Sian Smith
Designed by Victoria Bevan and Geoff Ward
Illustrated by Geoff Ward
Picture Research by Mica Brancic

Originated by Modern Age
Printed and bound in China by Leo Paper Group

13 12 11 10 09
10 9 8 7 6 5 4 3 2 1

**Library of Congress Cataloging-in-Publication
Data**
Solway, Andrew.
  Graphing changing landscapes / Andrew Solway.
-- 1st ed.
    p. cm. -- (Real world data)
  Includes bibliographical references and index.
  ISBN 978-1-4329-1528-5 (hc) -- ISBN 978-1-
4329-1543-8 (pb)
 1. Graphic methods. 2. Geology. 3. Landscape
changes. I. Title.
  QA90.S649 2008
  550.72'8--dc22
                                    2008018276

Acknowledgments
The publishers would like to thank the following
for permission to reproduce photographs:
© Alamy pp.**8** (Graham Bell), **23** (FLPA); © Corbis
pp.**12**, **4** (O. Alamany & E. Vicens), **6** (epa), **9**
(Naturfoto Honal), **10** (Michael Freeman), **14**
(Bob Krist), **15** (Momatiuk- Eastcott), **16** (zefa,
José Fuste Raga), **18** (Francesc Muntada), **22**
(Galen Rowell), **24** (Bill Ross), **27** (Lowell
Georgia); © NASA (GSFC, METI, ERSDAC,
JAROS and U.S./Japan ASTER Science Team)
p.**13**; © Photolibrary Group (Australian Only,
Stefan Mokrzecki) p.**26**

Cover photograph of East Beckwith Mountain,
reproduced with permission of ©Getty Images
(Minden Pictures, Tim Fitzharris).

Every effort has been made to contact copyright
holders of any material reproduced in this book.
Any omissions will be rectified in subsequent
printings if notice is given to the publishers.

The publishers would like to thank Harold Pratt for
his assistance in the preparation of this book.

CONTENTS

Some words are printed in bold, **like this**. You can find out what they mean by looking in the glossary, on page 30.

What type of landscape do you live in? Do you live in the mountains, or on a flat plain? Maybe you live on the coast, or by a river or lake. Mountains, plains, rivers, and lakes are all examples of **landforms**.

Whatever type of landscape you live in, its characteristics come from the rocks beneath the surface. They might be hard or soft. They could allow water through them or be impermeable (waterproof). In some places, there is mainly one type of rock. In other areas there are several different types of rock together. All these variations show as differences in the landscape.

Slow changes

The landforms around us seem fixed, but in fact they are changing very slowly. Rivers dig out valleys and flood plains. The weather gradually wears away mountains. Volcanoes pour out **lava**, which cools to become new rock. River **deltas** form new land as they fill up with mud and **silt**.

If we want to understand landforms, we have to understand how they form and how they change. You can learn about these things in this book.

 Mountains such as the Pyrenees, in southwestern Europe, are among the world's most spectacular landforms. They form when the rocks forming Earth's surface crumple and buckle.

Graphs and charts

Graphs and charts are ways to make sense of complex information by displaying it visually. One of the simplest types of graph is a bar chart. It is a good way to show the relationship between things that do not directly affect each other. The table and bar chart below show the areas of the continents. (1 square kilometer equals 0.39 square mile.) The tallest bar indicates the largest continent (Asia). The horizontal line across the bottom is the **x-axis**, where each continent is listed. The vertical line on the left , which shows the area, is the **y-axis**.

Continent	Area (000 km²)
Asia	44,614
Africa	30,319
North and Central America	24,247
South America	17,834
Europe	10,600
Antarctica	14,000
Australia	8,504

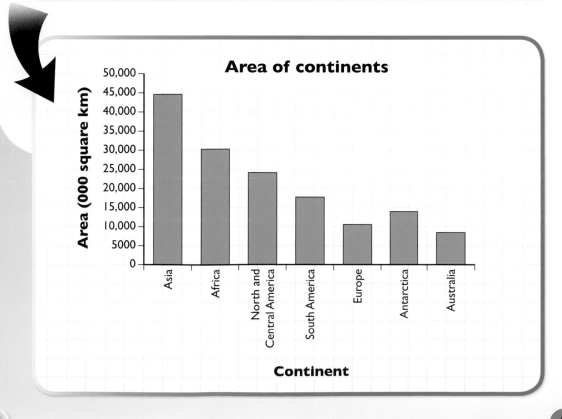

Area of continents

MAKING ROCKS

Have you seen film of a volcano erupting? Bright orange **lava** shoots out of the top and flows down its sides. The lava is so hot that it destroys everything in its path. But after some time, the lava begins to cool. Eventually, after weeks, months, or even years, the lava cools completely, leaving a layer of new rock.

Fiery rocks

Lava is one example of **igneous** rock. ("Igneous" means "fiery.") All igneous rock is formed when older rocks or pieces of rock melt. When the molten material cools again, it forms new rock.

Molten rock on the surface is called lava. When lava cools, it forms rocks such as basalt, pumice, and obsidian.

Sometimes molten rock forms underground and does not reach the surface. Underground molten rock is called **magma**. It cools more slowly than lava at the surface. It forms rocks such as granite and gabbro.

Lava flows from Kilauea volcano in Hawaii. Kilauea is the youngest volcano on Hawaii's Big Island. It is one of the most active volcanoes in the world.

Central furnace

Where does the heat to melt rocks come from? The center of Earth is very hot—between 6,000 and 7,000 °C (10,832 and 12,632 °F). This is four to five times hotter than a steel furnace. The heat is mostly left over from when Earth formed, billions of years ago. Heat is also produced by radioactivity in the rocks.

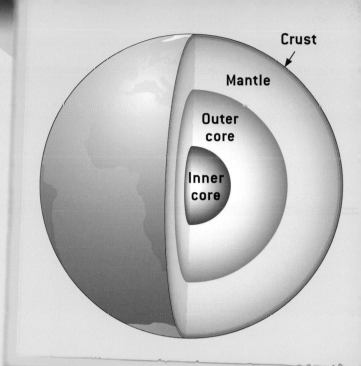

Crust
Mantle
Outer core
Inner core

Rock structure
Most rocks are made up of tiny crystals. In igneous rocks that form on the surface, such as basalt and pumice, the crystals are very tiny, like fine powder. Igneous rocks that form underground, such as granite, have bigger crystal pieces. In granite, you can see the different parts that make up the rock.

 This cross-section of Earth shows the layers that lie beneath the surface.

 This line graph shows the temperature at different depths below Earth's surface.

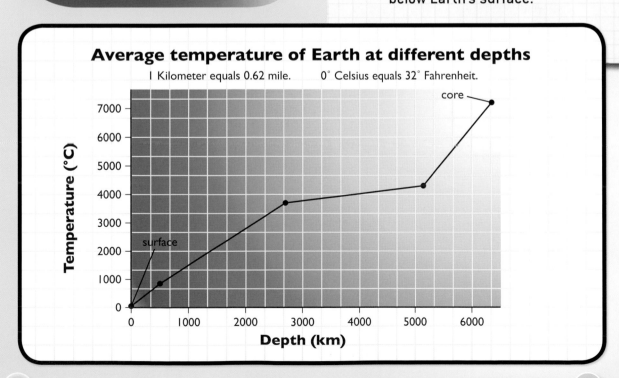

Average temperature of Earth at different depths

1 Kilometer equals 0.62 mile.   0° Celsius equals 32° Fahrenheit.

core

surface

Temperature (°C)

Depth (km)

Not all new rocks are formed when molten rock hardens. There are two other types of rock, known as **sedimentary** and **metamorphic**.

Layers of mud and sand

As their name suggests, sedimentary rocks form from sediments—materials such as sand, **silt**, or mud. Sediments build up in lakes, in slow-flowing parts of rivers, and on the seabed. As layers of sediment build up, the lower layers are crushed. Water is squeezed out, and **chemical reactions** bind the grains together to form sedimentary rock. Sandstone, limestone, coal, and shale are all types of sedimentary rock.

Most rocks are made from bits of other rocks, but limestone, chalk, and coal are different. The sediments that make up these rocks are largely the remains of living things. Limestone and chalk are largely made up of the shells of tiny sea creatures. Coal is made mainly of the remains of plants.

Metamorphosis

The third type of rock is known as metamorphic rock. "Metamorphosis" means "transformation," or change. Metamorphic rocks form from other rocks by a process of transformation. If an area of sedimentary or **igneous** rock is pushed deep underground, or gets close to an area of molten rock, it can get crushed and very hot (but not hot enough to melt). The combination of heat and **pressure** transform it into metamorphic rock. Metamorphic rocks include slate (from shale), marble (from limestone), and anthracite (from coal).

Because of the way they are laid down, sedimentary rocks form layers, or **strata**. The strata are clearly visible in this cliff in south Wales, in the United Kingdom.

Fossils

Sedimentary rocks often contain **fossils**. These are the bones, shells, or other hard parts of living things that were buried in the sediments that formed the rock. The bones or other parts may turn to rock, or they may leave an impression in the rocks.

 Limestone is often packed with fossils. Limestone is mainly made from the shells of billions of sea creatures.

Pie charts

Pie charts are a good way to show how something is divided up. Each piece of the circle, or "slice" of the pie, is a percentage of the whole. All the rocks in the world are made from a few simple chemicals. This pie chart shows the most common of these chemicals. You can see that silica (sand) and alumina together make up three-quarters of all rocks.

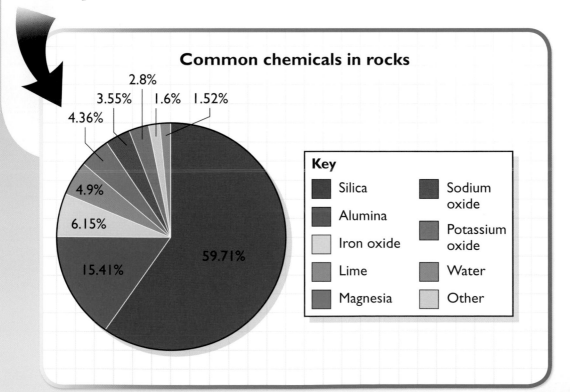

Common chemicals in rocks

2.8%
3.55% 1.6% 1.52%
4.36%
4.9%
6.15%
15.41%
59.71%

Key
- Silica
- Alumina
- Iron oxide
- Lime
- Magnesia
- Sodium oxide
- Potassium oxide
- Water
- Other

BREAKING ROCKS

Many **landforms** are made by the gradual wearing away of rock, rather than by new rock forming. The process by which rocks wear away is called **weathering**.

Wind and rain

In hot, dry places, wind is one of the main causes of weathering. The wind blows dust, sand, and grit against the rocks, and they scrape at the surface like sandpaper. Small pieces of rock break off as a result.

In wetter areas, rain is more likely to produce weathering. Rocks such as limestone weather quite quickly, because **chemical reactions** between the rock and rainwater gradually **dissolve** away the rock.

Heat and cold

Another way rocks are weathered is by heating and cooling. When rocks heat up, they expand a little, and when they cool they contract (shrink). Repeated expansion and contraction can cause cracks in the rock. Water gets into the cracks, and if the weather gets cold, it may freeze. Water expands as it freezes, so if the water freezes it opens up the cracks further. Eventually, pieces of rock break off.

The shapes of this **canyon** in Arizona were formed by water and wind. **Flash floods** have dug out the deep canyon, while winds have sculpted its sides.

The power of plants

Weathering is not always caused by the weather. Have you ever seen pavement lifted and cracked by tree roots? If so, you will understand how powerful plant roots can be. A tree or other plant growing on a rocky hillside or cliff can force open tiny cracks and break off pieces of rock.

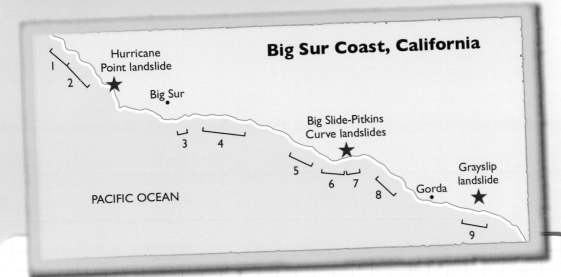

Big Sur Coast, California

Hurricane Point landslide

Big Sur

Big Slide-Pitkins Curve landslides

Grayslip landslide

Gorda

PACIFIC OCEAN

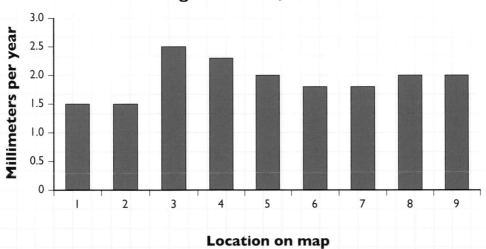

Average rate of cliff weathering along Big Sur Coast, California

Millimeters per year

Location on map

 The pounding of the sea often wears away at the coast. The shape of the coastline and the types of rock affect the speed at which this happens. This bar chart shows weathering rates for a part of the California coast. (1 millimeter equals 0.04 inch.) The rock is more **igneous** toward the north and more **sedimentary** toward the south.

EROSION AND DEPOSITION

People often use the word "**erosion**" to mean the wearing away of the landscape. Strictly speaking, this is not correct. **Weathering** wears away at the landscape. Erosion is the movement of the material that has been weathered.

Erosion usually happens initially through **gravity**. Pieces of rock that break from a steep slope or a cliff fall to the bottom and form a jumble of rock pieces known as **scree**.

Once pieces of rock have fallen to the ground, they may be carried by the wind, if they are small enough, or washed by the rain into streams and rivers. These streams and rivers carry away the material farther downstream.

 Cape Cod, off Massachusetts, shows evidence of erosion and deposition. Waves from the east (right) erode the eastern coast, but the sediments eroded are carried north and south to form a spit (top) and barrier islands (bottom).

spit

barrier islands

This satellite picture shows the mouth of the Hugli River in India. It shows clearly the brown sediment being deposited as the river discharges into the sea.

Deposition

All the pieces of rock or soil that are eroded from one place are eventually deposited in another. This is called **deposition**. Sand and dust carried by the wind falls to the ground when the wind drops. Pieces of rock, sand, and sediment that are eroded by rivers and streams eventually fall to the stream or riverbed. Smaller pieces are carried farther than larger ones. The sediments build up and gradually form new layers of **sedimentary** rock.

River deltas

At the mouth of many rivers, most of the river's remaining sediment is deposited, because the current has slowed down. As more sediment is deposited, the river channel can become completely blocked. The river then has to find a new route to the sea. This happens many times, so that eventually the river mouth becomes a maze of channels spreading out in a triangle from the main river channel. This is known as a **delta**.

RIVERS AND STREAMS

A large part of the landscape is formed by water. Running water flows downhill from mountains and hills, forming channels in the rock and soil as it flows. Over many years, the water erodes away the rock and forms deep valleys.

River features

Most rivers begin as rushing streams in mountainous areas. Water from many streams (tributaries) combines to form a river. Rivers usually flow through flatter areas as they near the coast. In these areas the river channel winds around (meanders), as the water finds the easiest path to the sea.

Sometimes a shift in the ground can produce a **fault**, creating a "step" in the ground. A waterfall results if a river flows over the fault. Often there is a layer of hard rock on the top of a waterfall, with softer rock below. The falling water undercuts the hard rock of the lip and creates a deep "plunge pool" below the fall.

 This shows the winding channels of Ox Bow River, Alaska. The loop of river in the center will eventually be cut off to form an oxbow lake.

 The Grand **Canyon** was formed by the Colorado River.

Which river is biggest?

We all know that the Nile River in Africa is the world's longest river. However, is the longest river really the biggest? In terms of the amount of water flowing down it, the Amazon in South America is definitely the biggest. It carries more water than the seven next biggest rivers put together! In terms of water flow, the Nile is not even in the top ten.

The Amazon is also biggest in terms of its drainage basin (the area of land whose water drains into a river). The Nile is third biggest using this measurement. The pictogram below shows the top six rivers in terms of the size of their drainage basin. (1 square kilometer equals 0.39 square mile.)

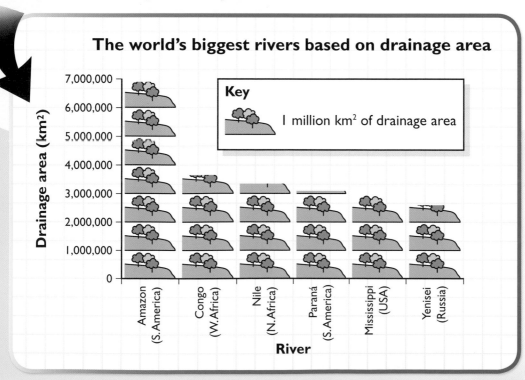

The world's biggest rivers based on drainage area

Key: 🌲 1 million km² of drainage area

Drainage area (km²) — River: Amazon (S. America), Congo (W. Africa), Nile (N. Africa), Paraná (S. America), Mississippi (USA), Yenisei (Russia)

Where land and sea meet, the sea shapes the coast. In some places, the sea wears away the shoreline. In others, it makes new land.

Headlands and bays

The types of rock along the coast affect the shape that a coastline takes. In places where the rock is softer, the coast erodes more quickly and a bay forms. The **headlands** on either side of the bay are made from harder rock that wears away more slowly.

Cliffs are often found along the coast. Waves attack the bottom of the cliff and gradually cut a notch in the cliff face. When this becomes deep enough, the cliff face above collapses. In this way, cliff faces gradually move backward.

Wave action can make all kinds of **landforms** along a rocky coast. If the waves beat against a crack in the rocks, a cave may gradually form. If the cave is on a headland, it may eventually wear through to form an arch. The arch gradually grows bigger, and finally the top collapses, leaving a pillar or "stack."

This stack and arch were formed by the action of the ocean at Etretat, Normandy, France.

Sand and pebbles

Waves can also deposit material rather than washing it away. In places such as the inner parts of bays, the waves may deposit material to form a beach. Beaches are either mostly sand or mostly shingle (pebbles).

Sometimes sand or pebbles are deposited so they extend out into the sea, rather than forming a beach. This is known as a spit. If a spit grows and becomes permanent, a sheltered stretch of water is formed behind it. This area can become mud flats or salt marsh.

Graphs and keys

This graph shows the six longest beaches in the world. (1 kilometer equals 0.62 mile.) The names of the beaches are too long to fit on the **x-axis**, so they are listed separately, in a **key**. A key can be a useful way to show information that cannot be clearly written directly on the graph.

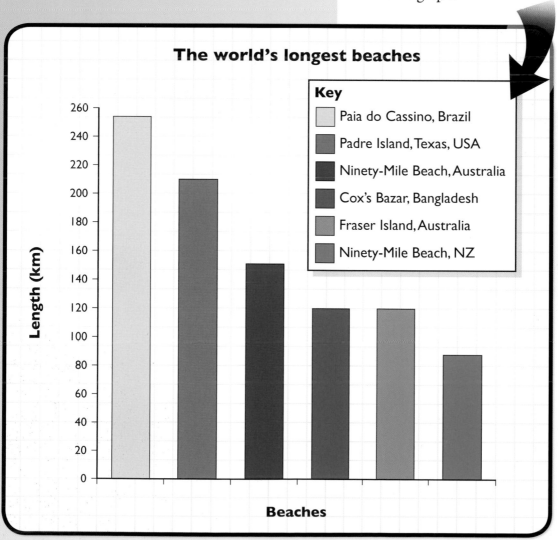

The world's longest beaches

Key
- Paia do Cassino, Brazil
- Padre Island, Texas, USA
- Ninety-Mile Beach, Australia
- Cox's Bazar, Bangladesh
- Fraser Island, Australia
- Ninety-Mile Beach, NZ

Length (km)

Beaches

Glaciers are huge rivers of ice. Like other rivers, they flow downhill, but very slowly. About 10,000 years ago, in the last **Ice Age**, glaciers covered about one-third of the land. Today, most of them have melted. However, the effects on the landscape can still be seen. Glaciers have carved out some of the most spectacular landscapes in the world.

Valleys, cirques, and arêtes

Valleys that once had glaciers in them look very different from other valleys. A normal valley is V-shaped, but glaciated valleys are U-shaped, with a flat base and steep sides.

In high hills and mountains, where the glaciers started, they leave behind other **landforms**. A glacier often starts in a steep-sided hollow, in the mountainside, called a **cirque** or **corrie**. When the glacier melts, it often leaves behind a lake or "tarn" in the cirque.

In some places, two glaciers flow in the same direction, side by side. As the glaciers grow and gradually wear away the rock, they create a knife-edged ridge called an arête.

 Valleys that once held glaciers have steep sides and a flattened bottom. Rivers flowing into the main valley sometimes enter high on its sides, forming what is known as a hanging valley.

Drowned valleys

During the last Ice Age, more of Earth's water was captive in glaciers than today. As a result, the sea level was lower. Glaciers in Norway and New Zealand carved out very deep, U-shaped valleys that ran to the sea.

As the climate got warmer and the glaciers melted, the sea level began to rise. The sea flooded into the deep coastal valleys to form narrow, steep-sided fjords.

Line graphs

Line graphs are good for showing sets of related information or for showing how something changes over time. Like all line graphs, this graph was drawn by plotting **data** points and connecting these with a line. But because the line is the same thickness as the points, it is hard to see them here. This graph shows how the volume of glaciers worldwide has changed since 1960. (1 square kilometer equals 0.39 square mile.) The values on the **y-axis** are negative because the glaciers are shrinking, rather than growing. This is because of **global warming**.

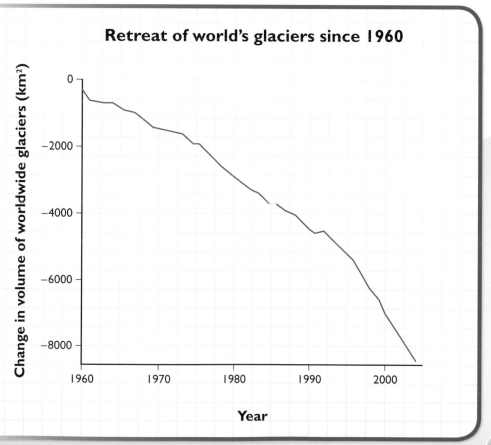

Retreat of world's glaciers since 1960

COLLIDING CONTINENTS

Weathering, **erosion**, and **deposition** are not the only processes that shape the landscape. Other processes happening deep beneath our feet can change the shape of continents, produce mountains and volcanoes, or create new land.

Moving plates

The rocks beneath our feet are only a thin skin on Earth's surface. This is called the **crust**. Below is a much thicker layer of very hot rocks, called the **mantle**. The top of the mantle is solid, but the lower part is **viscous**, like honey or syrup. The crust and the solid part of the mantle float on the viscous mantle rocks.

The crust is cracked and split into huge pieces known as **plates**. The main plates carry most of a continent or an ocean. They move around as they are dragged by slow currents in the mantle below.

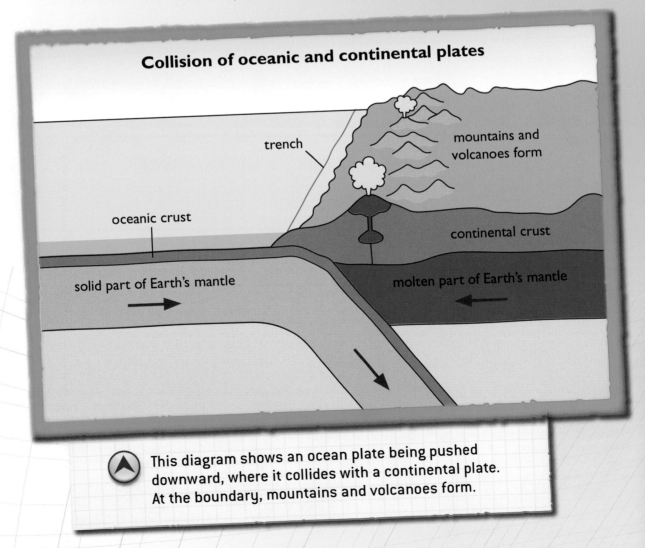

Collision of oceanic and continental plates

trench

mountains and volcanoes form

oceanic crust

continental crust

solid part of Earth's mantle

molten part of Earth's mantle

This diagram shows an ocean plate being pushed downward, where it collides with a continental plate. At the boundary, mountains and volcanoes form.

Where plates meet

Plates move very slowly—a few inches per year. Some plates are moving apart, while others are colliding. As plates move apart, new crust forms at the boundary. When plates collide, the edge of one plate slides beneath the other. The edges of the plates crumple, the whole land area is lifted up, and mountain ranges form. The Andes in South America formed in this way. There are many volcanoes along the plate boundary, where cracks and **faults** allow **magma** to rise to the surface.

Crust thickness

Earth's crust is thinnest on the ocean floor. Here it is about 5 kilometers (3 miles) thick. The rocks here are fairly recent, formed as plates moved apart. Continental crust is older and thicker. Most continental crust is around 30 kilometers (19 miles) thick, but in places it reaches 70 kilometers (43 miles). This bar chart shows how thick the crust is in the places shown on the map. (1 kilometer equals 0.62 mile.)

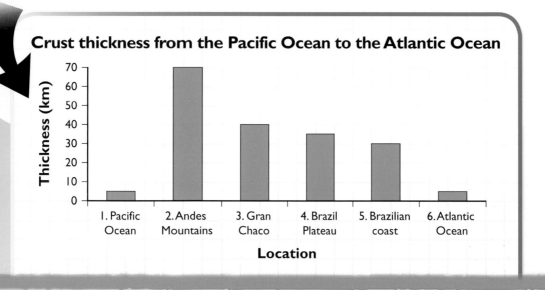

Crust thickness from the Pacific Ocean to the Atlantic Ocean

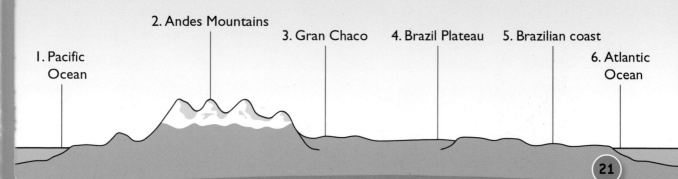

Cross-section of the crust of South America

MOUNTAINS AND VOLCANOES

Mountains are the most spectacular **landforms** on Earth. They usually form when two continental **plates** collide (see page 21). The type of mountain range that is formed depends partly on the rocks in the area. In some cases the rocks crumple to create fold mountains. Most large mountain ranges, such as the Rockies or the Himalayas, are fold mountains. In other cases the rocks **fault** (break and slip), rather than folding, to form block mountains.

Mountain ranges take hundreds of thousands of years to form. Even as they are forming, the processes of **weathering** and **erosion** are beginning to wear them down. Young mountains are tall and "craggy," with sharp peaks and steep slopes. As they get older, mountains are worn into lower, more rounded shapes. The Appalachians in North America are an old mountain range.

Volcanoes

Volcanoes are places where hot **lava** from deep underground bursts onto Earth's surface. A large volcanic eruption is unimaginably powerful, hurling hot rock and ash several miles into the air. An eruption can completely change an area, covering up the existing rocks and creating a barren wasteland. However, it is not long before plants and animals begin to live in the area again.

 The Karakoram Mountains in Pakistan are some of the highest and most rugged in the world.

Bursting from the sea

Many hot spots are under the ocean, because this is where Earth's **crust** is thinnest. Some underwater volcanoes grow so big that the tops rise out of the water, forming islands. The Hawaiian islands were formed this way.

 The island of Surtsey, near Iceland, was formed by a volcano erupting on the seabed. The island emerged from the sea in 1963.

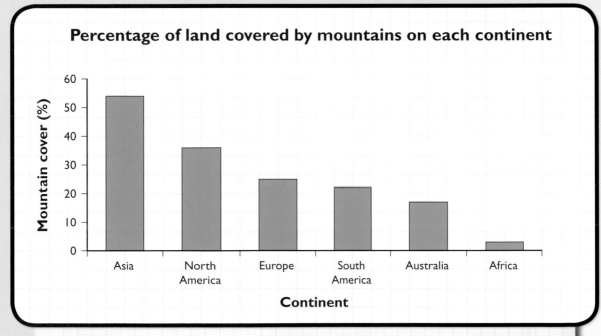

Percentage of land covered by mountains on each continent

Bar chart with Y-axis labeled "Mountain cover (%)" ranging from 0 to 60, and X-axis labeled "Continent".

Continent	Mountain cover (%)
Asia	54
North America	36
Europe	25
South America	22
Australia	17
Africa	3

 This bar chart shows how mountainous the different continents are. Asia is the most mountainous continent, and Africa the least.

THE ROCK CYCLE

Over millions of years, rocks are repeatedly weathered, eroded, and deposited to form new rocks. As the rocks change, the landscape is reshaped. This process is called the rock cycle.

 Devil's Tower in Wyoming is a **landform** known as a volcanic plug. It originally formed inside a volcano, when **lava** hardened and blocked up the volcano. Over millions of years, the softer sandstone that formed the outside of the volcano was worn away, leaving the hard rock within.

The rock cycle

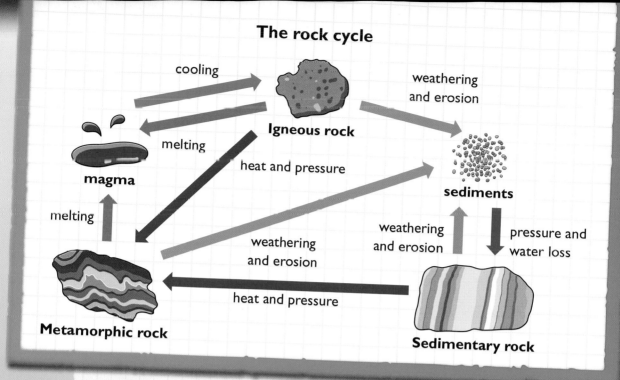

The rock cycle shows the many different ways that one type of rock can turn into another.

A cycle of changes

Rocks can break down and change in many ways. The series of steps outlined below represents just one version of the rock cycle—there are many others.

1 Underground, a pocket of **magma** slowly cools to form **igneous** rock. Over time the rocks above the igneous rock are worn away, exposing the igneous rock.

2 The igneous rock is slowly weathered, then **gravity** and water carry the pieces away. The smaller pieces are carried downriver and deposited on the seabed. They become part of a layer of **sedimentary** rock.

3 At some point a large amount of magma pushes up from below into the sedimentary layer. The rock around the magma does not melt, but it is heated and squeezed. It changes to **metamorphic** rock.

4 Movements in giant **plates** that make up Earth's **crust** (see pages 20–21) cause the metamorphic rock to be pushed deep underground. Here it melts to form magma.

5 The magma pushes up through cracks in the rocks until it is close to the surface. Here it cools and once again forms igneous rock.

6 The igneous rock reaches the surface through **erosion**, or by being pushed up by **tectonic** movements. The cycle has started once again.

THE CHANGING EARTH

The landscape around us looks fixed and unchanging. But as we have learned, it is anything but. A range of hills may start out as a layer of sediment on the seabed. It could then become tall, rugged mountains before being worn down to rounded hills.

Agents of change

A few processes are responsible for most of the changes that create and shape **landforms**. Rain, wind, and temperature changes cause **weathering** and **erosion**. These break down rocks in one place, then move the remains and deposit them somewhere else. **Tectonic** movements can create an ocean between two land areas or create land where once there was sea. Along the edges of **plates**, mountains and volcanoes form.

Changing rocks

As landforms change, the rocks that they are made of change, too. **Igneous** and **metamorphic** rocks turn into sediments, which in time become **sedimentary** rocks. Sedimentary rocks become buried underground, where they may turn into metamorphic or igneous rocks. These changes are happening all the time.

 These rounded granite boulders in Australia are called the "Devil's marbles." They are formed by the splitting and rounding off of large blocks of rock through weathering.

 Landscapes usually change slowly, but this part of the coast in Chesapeake Bay, in the eastern United States, is eroding rapidly. Within a year or two, these houses will have fallen into the sea.

Noticing changes

Landscapes around the world continue to change. A few changes happen fast enough for us to see them. Volcanoes, landslides, and mudslides can produce changes very quickly. In places where the coast is eroding fast, we can see the changes over a period of years. Other changes are slower, but measurable. We cannot see the continental plates move, or the ocean plates spread, but we can measure the small changes using scientific instruments.

Even the tiniest changes have a big effect over a long time period. So, how will the world look in 10 million years? Would we recognize it?

Data is information about something. We often get important data as a mass of numbers, and it is difficult to make any sense of them. Graphs and charts are ways of displaying information visually. This helps us to see relationships and patterns in the data. Different types of graphs or charts are good for displaying different types of information.

Bar charts

A bar graph is good for comparing groups of things. The different groups or categories are named along the bottom of the graph. Up the side is what is being measured. The height of each bar is the amount of each measurement. A bar chart can have two of three sets of bars or several bars stacked on top of each other.

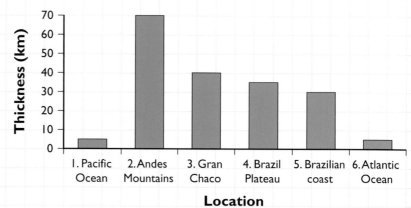

Crust thickness from the Pacific Ocean to the Atlantic Ocean

Thickness (km)

1. Pacific Ocean
2. Andes Mountains
3. Gran Chaco
4. Brazil Plateau
5. Brazilian coast
6. Atlantic Ocean

Location

Pictograms

A pictogram is like a bar chart, but it has pictures or symbols instead of solid bars.

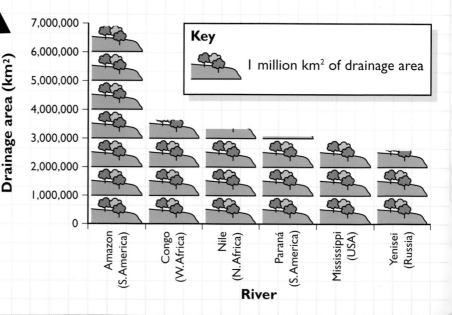

The world's biggest rivers based on drainage area

Drainage area (km^2)

Key
1 million km^2 of drainage area

Amazon (S. America)
Congo (W. Africa)
Nile (N. Africa)
Paraná (S. America)
Mississippi (USA)
Yenisei (Russia)

River

Line graphs

A line graph is best for showing connected information. For example, if the same thing is measured at different points, the results are best shown on a line graph.

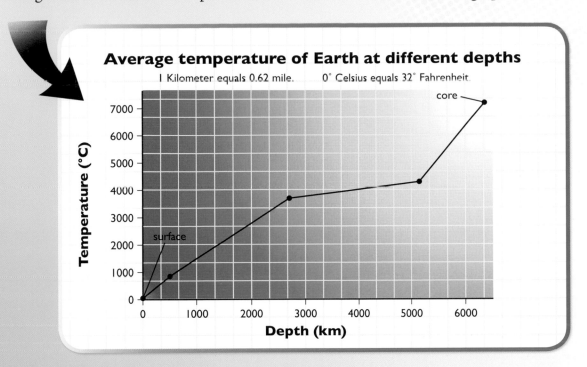

Average temperature of Earth at different depths

I Kilometer equals 0.62 mile.   0° Celsius equals 32° Fahrenheit.

core

surface

Temperature (°C)

Depth (km)

Pie charts

A pie chart is the best way to show how something is divided up. The "pie" is a circle, and each slice of the pie is a wedge. The size of the wedge shows how much of the whole that slice is.

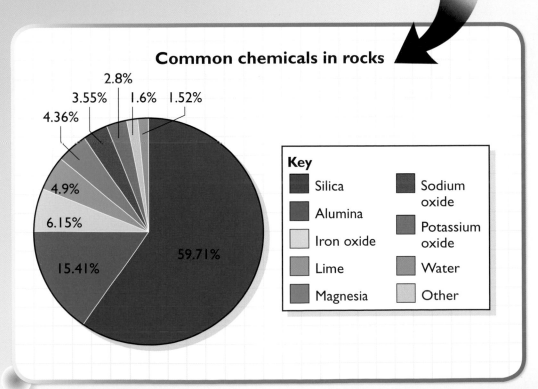

Common chemicals in rocks

2.8%
3.55%   1.6%   1.52%
4.36%
4.9%
6.15%
15.41%
59.71%

Key

- Silica
- Alumina
- Iron oxide
- Lime
- Magnesia
- Sodium oxide
- Potassium oxide
- Water
- Other

GLOSSARY

canyon deep river valley with steep sides

chemical reaction interaction between two substances that causes them to change

crust layer of solid rock that covers Earth's surface

cirque bowl-shaped depression scraped out of a mountainside by a glacier

corrie bowl-shaped depression scraped out of a mountainside by a glacier

data information, often in the form of numbers

delta (river) fan-shaped area at the mouth of a river, where the water flows along a number of channels between deposits of sand, silt, or mud

deposition when sand, mud, or other sediments are deposited (dropped) on the bed of a river, lake, or the sea

dissolve to mix a substance completely with water so that it is no longer visible

erosion movement of pieces of rock or soil that have been weathered from the surface

fault shift or gap in the rocks of an area

fjord deep, steep-sided flooded valley on the coast

flash flood sudden flood of water along a river channel caused by heavy rains

fossil remains of a living thing either turned to rock or that has left its shape in rock

global warming slight increase in the average temperature of the air in the atmosphere over the last few decades

gravity constant force that pulls all things toward Earth

headland piece of land that sticks out into the sea

Ice Age period in the past when the climate was colder than it is today and snow and ice covered many areas

igneous any rock formed by the cooling of lava or magma

key something that shows what symbols or colors on a graph stand for

landform feature of the landscape such as mountain, valley, river, plain, or cliff

lava molten rock on Earth's surface

magma molten rock below ground

mantle thick layer of very hot, partly molten rock that lies underneath Earth's crust

metamorphic type of rock that forms from other rocks by a combination of heating (but not melting) and pressure

plate huge section of Earth's crust that is able to move in relation to other parts of the crust

pressure crushing force

scree area of broken rock collected at the bottom of a cliff or steep slope

sedimentary type of rock formed when layers of sediments such as sand or mud are compacted (squeezed) for long periods

silt very fine type of sediment—very tiny particles of rock

stratum (plural: strata) layer of rock

tectonic tectonic movement is the movement of the plates on Earth's surface on the thick, liquid rocks of the mantle

viscous thick like honey or syrup

weathering breaking of pieces of rock or soil from Earth's surface

x-axis horizontal line on a graph

y-axis vertical line on a graph

FURTHER INFORMATION

Books

Cryute, Clay. *Tales of a Prehistoric Sponge: The Rock Cycle*. Chicago: Raintree, 2006.

Harman, Rebecca. *Rock Cycles: Formation, Properties, and Erosion*. Chicago: Heinemann Library, 2005.

Nadeau, Isaac. *Library of Landforms: Glaciers*. New York: PowerKids, 2006.

Raum, Elizabeth. *World's Wonders: Landforms*. Chicago: Raintree, 2006.

Spilsbury, Louise and Richard. *The Disappearing Mountain and Other Earth Mysteries: Erosion and Weathering*. Chicago: Raintree, 2005.

Taylor, Barbara. *Geography Skills: Understanding Landforms*. Mankato, Minn.: Smart Apple Media, 2008.

Websites

This website has an interactive animation on the rock cycle.
www.classzone.com/books/earth_science/terc/content/investigations/es0602/es0602page02.cfm

This National Aeronautics and Space Administration (NASA) website has a multimedia history of Glacier Bay, Alaska.
http://glacier-bay.gsfc.nasa.gov/

Learn about the rock cycle, Earth's plates, and what rocks are made of.
www.windows.ucar.edu/tour/link=/earth/geology/geology.html

INDEX